The Wright
Brothers

Other titles in the Inventors and Creators series include:

Alexander Graham Bell
Walt Disney
Thomas Edison
Albert Einstein
Henry Ford
Benjamin Franklin
Jim Henson
J.K. Rowling
Jonas Salk
Dr. Seuss
Steven Spielberg

The Wright
Brothers

Sheila Wyborny

**KIDHAVEN
PRESS™**

THOMSON

GALE

SOUTH HUNTINGTON
PUBLIC LIBRARY
HUNTINGTON STATION, NY 11746

San Diego • Detroit • New York • San Francisco • Cleveland
New Haven, Conn. • Waterville, Maine • London • Munich

JB
Wright w

THOMSON
™
GALE

© 2003 by KidHaven Press. KidHaven Press is an imprint of The Gale Group, Inc.,
a division of Thomson Learning, Inc.

KidHaven™ and Thomson Learning™ are trademarks used herein under license.

For more information, contact
KidHaven Press
27500 Drake Rd.
Farmington Hills, MI 48331-3535
Or you can visit our Internet site at http://www.gale.com

ALL RIGHTS RESERVED.
No part of this work covered by the copyright hereon may be reproduced or used in any form
or by any means—graphic, electronic, or mechanical, including photocopying, recording, taping,
Web distribution or information storage retrieval systems—without the written permission of
the publisher.

LIBRARY OF CONGRESS CATALOGING-IN-PUBLICATION DATA

Wyborny, Sheila, 1950–
The Wright brothers / by Sheila Wyborny.
  p. cm.—(Inventors and creators)
Summary: Profiles Orville and Wilbur Wright, beginning with their childhoods in
the Midwest, covering their business enterprises, interest in aircraft, and
successful flights, and ending with a look at their legacy.
Includes bibliographical references and index.
  ISBN 0-7377-1369-0 (hardback : alk. paper)
1. Wright, Orville, 1871–1948—Juvenile literature. 2. Wright, Wilbur, 1867–1912—
Juvenile literature. 3. Aeronautics—United States—Biography—Juvenile literature.
[1. Wright, Orville, 1871–1948. 2. Wright, Wilbur, 1867–1912. 3. Aeronautics—
Biography.] I. Title. II. Series.
  TL540 .W7 W93 2003
  629.13'0092'273—dc21
                                                              2002009143

Printed in China

30652 001311929

Contents

From Dreams to Flight

The Wright brothers were not the only inventors who worked on developing the airplane, but they are the people credited with taking the airplane from the experimental stage to actual flight.

Beginning with man-carrying **gliders** flown on the windy shores of North Carolina's Outer Banks, Orville

A painting depicts the Wright brothers' first motorized flight at Kitty Hawk, North Carolina, in 1903.

The work of the Wright brothers made today's high-speed aircraft possible.

and Wilbur Wright created an engine-powered, heavier-than-air airplane that they taught themselves to fly.

They put their flyer through its paces before military officers, presidents, and kings of many countries, and showed nations that this wondrous flying machine could be a vehicle of transportation or a weapon of war.

Although Wilbur died before the airplane's full potential was realized, Orville lived to see airplanes used to transport deadly atomic bombs in World War II and to commercially transport hundreds of thousands of people all over the world.

Chapter One

The Bishop's Family

Orville and Wilbur Wright were two of seven children born to Susan and Milton Wright. Susan was the daughter of a German wagon and carriage maker. Milton, whose family came from England, was a bishop in the United Brethren Church, a small protestant group.

Family Traits

Orville and Wilbur had two older brothers, Reuchlin and Lorin; a younger sister, Katharine; and a twin brother and sister, Otis and Ida, who died in infancy. Wilbur was born on April 16, 1867, near Millville, Indiana, and Orville was born on August 19, 1871, in Dayton, Ohio.

As Bishop Wright was transferred from church to church, the family moved often. By the time the Wright children were adults, they had moved twelve times. Because of these frequent moves, the children learned to support and rely on each other and were much closer than children in other families.

Like children in most families, the Wright children learned from their parents. Susan Wright was an unusual mother, however. She was a talented mechanic and taught her children how to work with their hands. Mrs. Wright was handy with tools and did most of the household repairs. She designed and made her own clothes and made sleds and simple toys for the children.

Wilbur and Orville inherited their mother's mechanical aptitude, as well as her ability to craft items with their hands. Orville and Wilbur liked woodworking. Wilbur taught Orville how to make simple toys and, at the age of twelve, Orville learned wood **engraving**. He studied at the local library and made an engraving tool from the spring of a broken pocketknife.

Orville and Wilbur Wright practiced their woodworking skills in shops like this one.

Bishop Wright, on the other hand, could barely drive a nail. His skill was keeping records. He kept records of family activities and documented his family's history. From their father, the children inherited an eye for detail and keeping accurate records. These skills served Orville and Wilbur well in later years.

Both parents encouraged their children to use their time wisely. If the children wanted spending money, they had to earn it. But although they taught their children to work for their money, Bishop and Mrs. Wright were

The Wright brothers' childhood home in Dayton, Ohio.

very protective. They did not want anyone outside their faith influencing their children and kept a careful watch over their children's friendships.

Education and Inspiration

Susan and Milton Wright inspired the Wright children throughout their lives. The parents believed in equal rights for women and encouraged both their sons and their daughter to be free thinkers. If the children felt they had something more important or interesting to do than to go to school a certain day, they were allowed to miss school. But although their parents had a liberal attitude about attending school, they were great believers in education.

Bishop Wright taught his children to read the First McGuffy Reader, a reader that contained short, inspirational stories, before they started school at the age of five. The older children helped the younger children. Wilbur helped teach his younger brother, Orville, to read.

When Orville was five, he started kindergarten. His mother walked him to school that first day, but afterward he was expected to walk to school by himself. But Orville had other plans. Some weeks later, Mrs. Wright learned that Orville had gone to school only that first day. The rest of the time, he had spent the days with one of his friends.

After that, Orville attended school regularly, but he had his own ideas about how to spend class time. One day his teacher caught him playing with pieces of wood at his desk instead of doing his assignment. She asked him what he was doing. He replied that he was planning a flying machine, and that he and Wilbur would one day make and sell the machines.

It was not only Orville who was interested in flying machines, though. While on one of his frequent trips, their father bought them a rubber band–powered helicopter toy. Eleven-year-old Wilbur and seven-year-old Orville examined how it worked, and then made flying toys of their own. They later described the event: "Our first interest [in flight] began when we were children. Father brought home to us a small toy actuated by a rubber spring which would lift itself into the air."[1]

Wilbur was less outgoing than Orville, but he was very self-assured. He liked geography and history and was also good at math. He once convinced a teacher that she was wrong in marking one of his math answers incorrect. When she graded his paper again, she discovered she had made a mistake.

Change and Health Problems

In March 1885 when Wilbur was eighteen years old and preparing to go to college, a freak accident occurred that changed his life. While playing a game with his friends on a frozen lake, Wilbur was hit in the face with a hockey stick, which tore his lips and broke many of his teeth. Luckily, the accident happened near a retirement home, and the staff doctor on duty treated Wilbur right away. But although he received prompt treatment, Wilbur suffered years of pain. Shortly after his accident, he began having heart problems and suffering with stomach pain. Because of his health problems, he became depressed and withdrawn. This **depression** lasted more than four years.

As Wilbur slid into a world of pain and depression, Orville developed an interest in printing, working with an old printing press of his father's. In Orville's spare time, he printed circulars, posters, and pamphlets for customers. He was so successful that he changed some of his own plans for the future.

Wilbur (left) and Orville had different hobbies while growing up but shared an interest in flight.

Instead of returning to high school for his senior year, Orville went into business. By then he had learned a lot about printing and decided this was the career path he wanted to follow. He tried to get Wilbur interested in the printing business. Wilbur, still unwell, showed no particular interest. But soon a tragedy occurred that took Wilbur's mind off of his own problems.

A Family Tragedy

As early as 1883, Susan Wright had symptoms of **tuberculosis**. Over the next several years, her health began to fail. Wilbur rallied from his depression to care for his mother as she had cared for him after his injury. As her body weakened and she was no longer able to walk, Wilbur, ignoring his own pain, carried her down the stairs to the parlor every morning so she could take part in family life. Every evening he carried her back to her bedroom.

Susan Wright died in July 1889 at the age of fifty-eight. Milton Wright credited his son's loving care with extending his wife's life. He said of Wilbur: "Such devotion of a son has rarely been equaled, and the mother and son were fully able to appreciate each other. Her life was probably lengthened, at least two years, by his skill and assiduity."[2]

Though a tragedy, Susan Wright's death triggered Wilbur's return to the outside world, and Orville's enthusiasm for the printing business finally gained Wilbur's attention.

Chapter Two

Brothers in Business

Orville Wright was energetic and enthusiastic, with drive and determination. He was good at solving problems. However, he was not comfortable speaking in public. Wilbur, on the other hand, was a gifted public speaker, cool and controlled, but he still suffered from occasional bouts of depression. Because they knew one another's strengths and weaknesses so well, Orville and Wilbur thought they would work well together.

First Business Ventures

First, Orville went into business with his old school friend, Ed Sines. Wilbur joined them in 1889. Their business cards read "Wright Brothers: Job Printers at 7 Hawthorne Street." They printed directories, programs for banks, posters, cards, and letterheads.

In March 1899, they started their first newspaper, the *Westside News*. Wilbur was the editor, Orville was the publisher, and Ed Sines sold advertising. But soon they were dissatisfied with printing a weekly paper and wanted to do something more challenging. On April 5,

1890, they printed the final edition of the *Westside News* and on April 30, the *Evening Item,* a daily newspaper, was born.

At the same time, the Wright brothers briefly published a paper for the African American community. Another of Orville's classmates also worked for the printing company for a time. Paul Laurence Dunbar was an African American, the son of former slaves. His idea was to start a publication for African American people of Dayton. The paper was called the *Tattler.* But money was limited and they were not able to sell enough advertising to keep the paper going. Only three issues of the *Tattler* were printed.

The *Evening Item* did not last long, either. At that time, there were twelve newspapers in Dayton, and the Wright brothers did not have the money to compete with them. The final issue of the *Evening Item* was printed in August 1890. It lasted less than four months.

Problems in Partnership

Although they left the newspaper business, Orville and Wilbur remained in the printing business and were fairly successful. But their partnership was not without problems.

Although he had started the business, Orville sometimes felt he was treated more as a younger brother than as a business partner. The brothers had arguments. Fortunately, they could argue through their problems with a sense of humor. This helped them find solutions to many of their problems.

Paul Laurence Dunbar worked with the Wright brothers for a short time at their printing company.

Wilbur spoke of these conflicts: "I love to scrap [fight] with Orv. Orv is such a good scrapper."[3]

The printing business was doing well, but once again the Wright brothers looked ahead. They were ready for new challenges.

Bicycle Shop

With the printing business running smoothly, most of the work could be handled by Ed Sines. Orville and

Wilbur looked for another business that would challenge them and add to their income.

Orville bought a new bicycle called a safety bicycle and a short time later Wilbur bought one, also. The new type of bicycle had two wheels of the same size. The brothers liked their new bicycles and enjoyed riding around the back roads of Dayton in their spare time. Orville entered races and won some of them, but Wilbur continued to enjoy long, leisurely rides in the country.

The safety bicycle became popular. More and more people wanted bicycles, and the Wright brothers saw an opportunity for a new business. Late in the winter of 1892, they opened a bicycle repair shop and showroom across the street from the printing business. Although

The Wright brothers enjoyed riding safety bicycles like this one that was used during the 1896 Olympics.

Orville Wright (left) and one of his business partners, Ed Sines, work hard in their bicycle shop in 1897.

the business made a slow start, the Wright brothers were soon well known around Dayton as bicycle mechanics. But bicycles were expensive. To be really successful the Wrights had to find ways to make bicycles affordable. The average person's wages were $450 a year; a good bicycle cost $40 to $50. The Wrights sold the best brands and stressed quality. They arranged payment schedules for their customers and took old bicycles as trade-ins, much like modern automobile dealerships.

Business was so good throughout that first spring and summer season that they had to expand their quarters. It appeared that the Wrights had created another successful business.

Orville and Wilbur were close as brothers and as business partners. Both were bachelors and lived at home with their father and their sister. The brothers maintained a joint bank account, and they trusted each other with the money. Both could use the account, and both were free to withdraw money at any time without telling the other.

In the beginning, the future of their new business looked promising, but the Wrights still had much to learn about the bicycle business.

Problems and Opportunities

The brothers discovered that bicycling was a seasonal pastime. People enjoyed riding in the warm spring and summer months and into the early fall, but winters in Ohio often meant snow and ice, which was not good for riding.

Once, the Wrights borrowed money from their father. Wilbur wrote to Bishop Wright, who was on one of his trips for the church, keeping him up to date on his $150 investment:

> The bicycle business is fair. Selling new wheels is about done for this year, but the repairing business is good and we are getting about $20 a month from the rent of three wheels. . . . We have done so well renting them that we have held onto them instead of disposing of them at once, although we really need the money invested in them.[4]

In the slow seasons, they repaired the traded-in bicycles, and they later designed and built their own model, the Van Cleve, named after their pioneer ancestor.

The Wright Cycle Company building still stands today as a museum and historical site.

During one winter season, they published a weekly advertising brochure called "Snapshots at Current Events," a publication for cyclists. Naturally, they advertised their bicycle shop in the brochure.

With the printing business balancing with the solidly growing bicycle business, the Wright brothers could have slowed down and enjoyed their success. Throughout their young adult years, the Wrights focused their time and energies on developing their businesses rather than dating. Although they remained bachelors and did not have children of their own, they enjoyed entertaining their brothers' children. Life for the Wright brothers could have settled into a comfortable routine, but they wanted new challenges.

Chapter Three

Taking to the Skies

In 1896 Orville became ill with **typhoid fever** from drinking polluted water. He nearly died. Wilbur and Katharine nursed him through his illness. When his health began to improve, Wilbur looked for ways to keep Orville entertained.

Early Interests

During Orville's recovery, Wilbur read him stories about the late glider builder and pilot Otto Lilienthal. By the time Orville recovered, the brothers were so interested in flying that they looked for other books on the subject. They had found something else to help them occupy the slow winter months: studying flight.

They read everything they could find around Dayton about flying, but little was available. So they wrote to the Smithsonian Institution in Washington, D.C., and asked for articles about aviation. They were sent four pamphlets of aviation articles and a list of books: Samuel Langley's *Experiments in Aerodynamics of 1891*, Octave Chanute's *Progress in Flying Machines of 1894*, and James

Mean's *Aeronautical Annuals for 1895, 1896, and 1897*. The Wrights ordered the books and read them, over and over, during the winter.

After poring over all of the books and articles they could find, they decided that the most successful approach to flying had been Otto Lilienthal's. Lilienthal and his brother, Gustav, worked for more than twenty years on the problem of flying. Otto Lilienthal completed more than two thousand glides, sometimes reaching an altitude of sixty-five feet. Otto discovered one of the secrets of flight: A curved wing surface, where the air

Otto Lilienthal demonstrates the glider he created in 1893. A friend watches from below.

has farther to travel across the wing's top surface than its bottom surface, creates an **airfoil**, a shape that causes lift. But tragically, Otto Lilienthal died in a gliding accident.

Wilbur spoke of their frustration in those early days of gathering information: "At that time, there was no flying art in the proper sense of the word, but only a flying problem. Thousands of men had thought about flying machines and a few had even built machines which they called flying machines, but these were guilty of almost everything except flying."[5]

They continued searching for more information about flying and, in the winter of 1899, the brothers found a French book about how birds fly, *L'Empire de l'Air*, to add to their growing collection. Finally, the Wright brothers had gathered and studied all of the information they could find, and they were ready to move on to the next step: experimentation.

Making Plans

First, the Wright brothers built kite-sized models of gliders. While working in the bicycle shop one day, Wilbur discovered the answer to another flying problem. Lilienthal was killed in a gliding accident because the flow of air over the wing was disrupted, and Wilbur knew that Lilienthal tried to maintain control of the glider by shifting his weight from side to side. If Lilienthal had been able to control the shape of the glider's wings while in flight rather than having to try to force his weight from side to side to maintain balance and control, he probably would not have crashed. One day,

Engineers in a wind tunnel test a life-sized reproduction of a glider the Wright brothers designed in 1901.

Wilbur accidentally discovered a way to control the shape of a wing's surface. Wilbur was talking with a customer, twisting an oblong inner tube box in his hands. He twisted one end of the box in one direction and the other end in the opposite direction. If a pilot could twist the wings in a similar manner, the glider would maintain balance in the air. The Wrights attached cords to the ends of the wings of their glider kite and controlled the shape of the wings from the ground as their kite flew. Now it was time to take their experiments a step further.

They wanted to work with larger gliders that could carry a pilot. They needed a place with strong enough winds to hold the glider in the air. Wilbur wrote to writer and engineer Octave Chanute and asked about possible testing sites. "My business requires that my experimental work be confined to the months between September and January and I would be particularly thankful for advice as to a suitable locality where I could depend on winds of about 15 miles per hour without rain or too inclement weather."[6]

Wilbur intended to attach the glider to the top of a tower by a rope and pulley with a counterweight so the glider could float on the winds as it was hoisted up by the counterweight. Instead, Chanute suggested that sea breezes and sand hills would be safer for the glider and the pilot than being hoisted up a tower.

Choosing the Site

Chanute knew of several locations. Among them were the coasts of North Carolina, California, and Florida. But California and Florida were too far away, and so Orville and Wilbur decided that Kitty Hawk, on the coast of North Carolina, would be a good place to test their glider.

The site was selected, but they still needed the right materials to build the glider. Once again Wilbur wrote to Chanute, who told him that Cincinnati, Ohio, would be the best place to find the spruce wood Wilbur needed for the glider's **spars**. Chanute also sent a recipe for varnish for the wing covers.

Orville and Wilbur had a design, the right materials, and a good location to test their large glider. But getting to the site and then assembling the glider on-site would be difficult.

Experiments at Kitty Hawk

In September 1900 Wilbur traveled to Kitty Hawk. Orville remained behind for the last few weeks of the bicycle shop's fall business before joining his brother. The first part of Wilbur's journey took him to Elizabeth City, North Carolina. From there, the only way to reach Kitty Hawk was by boat. Unfortunately, the only boat available was leaky and not very sturdy. Wilbur later described part of the trip. "In a severe gust the foresail was blown loose

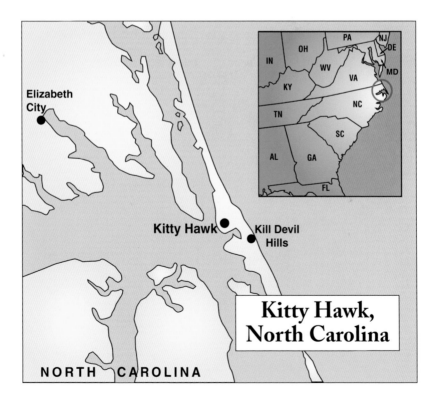

from the boom and fluttered to leeward with a terrible roar. The boy and I finally succeeded in taking it [the foresail] in though it was rather dangerous work in the dark with the boat rolling so badly."[7]

By the time Wilbur reached the island, he had not eaten for two days. Bill and Addie Tate, island residents, took pity on Wilbur, fed him, and gave him a place to sleep. The Tates and the Wrights remained friends for the rest of their lives.

Orville arrived in Kitty Hawk on Friday, September 28, 1900, with camping equipment, coffee, tea, sugar, and other supplies.

The Wrights' first full-sized glider was assembled under a canvas tarp in the Tate's front yard. Wilbur used Addie's sewing machine to restitch the fabric wing coverings to fit sixteen-foot spars, because he had been un-

One of the Wright brothers drags out glider equipment at their campsite in Kitty Hawk, North Carolina.

Two assistants launch Wilbur Wright in his glider at Kill Devil Hills, North Carolina, in 1901.

able to find eighteen-foot spars, for which the original wing coverings had been made. The **wing-warping** lines were attached to a hip cradle, which the pilot would control by shifting his body from side to side. The finished glider weighed about fifty pounds.

When the Wrights moved to their campsite, they faced a number of hardships. They were tormented by mosquitoes, and the brothers burned tree stumps to ward them off. The smoke made them cough and made their eyes water, but smoke was better than mosquitoes. High winds were also a problem. Once, a storm came through that lasted two days. The Wrights remained

A pilot operates a modern hang glider using methods similar to those the Wright brothers pioneered.

huddled in their tent throughout much of the storm as the wind shook its roof and sides. Once the storm was over, Orville and Wilbur had to dig out the glider, which was buried under the blowing sand. There were also occasional crashes, resulting in a number of bumps, cuts, and bruises to the pilots.

Despite problems, they continued to fly their glider, both manned and unmanned. Wilbur's first test flight reached an altitude of fifteen feet.

On the last day of their first series of glider flights, they traveled four miles south of Kitty Hawk to Kill Devil Hills, where there were higher dunes and fewer beachcombers, who could get in the way.

Looking Beyond Gliders

Altogether, the Wright brothers made three trips to the coast of North Carolina to test their gliders. With each trip, they made changes in their design to improve the gliders' flights. By their third trip, Wilbur had spent the longest time in the air, at twenty-six seconds.

Orville and Wilbur were now seasoned glider pilots, but already they looked toward a new challenge. They intended to design, build, and fly a heavier-than-air aircraft.

Chapter Four

Flight and Beyond

The Wright brothers learned much during their three seasons of flying gliders, but the gliders were merely a step toward their goal. Gliders depended upon strong winds to keep them in the air. But the Wrights wanted to design and build a craft that would not be totally at the mercy of the winds.

First Powered Flight

The Wrights designed a **biplane** with an engine. The craft could take off, travel, and land under its own power. One of their design plans was the balance of the aircraft. For their motorized aircraft, the Wright brothers placed the engine to the pilot's right and balanced the extra weight by making the right wing four inches longer than the left. They mounted the engine beside—instead of behind—the pilot in case of a crash. At 179 pounds, a rear-mounted engine could crush the pilot.

The design also included two **propellers**. The spinning of a single propeller creates torque, a twisting movement of the craft in the direction opposite to the direction the propeller is spinning. By having two pro-pellers spinning in opposite directions, the torque would be neutralized.

Once the aircraft's parts were ready, the Wrights re-turned to the Outer Banks of North Carolina at Kill Devil Hills, but again were plagued by bad weather. Wilbur described one stormy day as Orville attempted repairs: Orville "quickly mounted to the edge of the roof when the wind caught under his coat and folded it back over his head. As the hammer and nails were in his pocket and up over his head, he was unable to get his hands on them."[8]

They finished building the aircraft on-site and pre-pared for their test flights. The first trial was on Monday, December 14, 1903, a downhill launch at Kill Devil Hills. But poor wind conditions caused the craft to stall

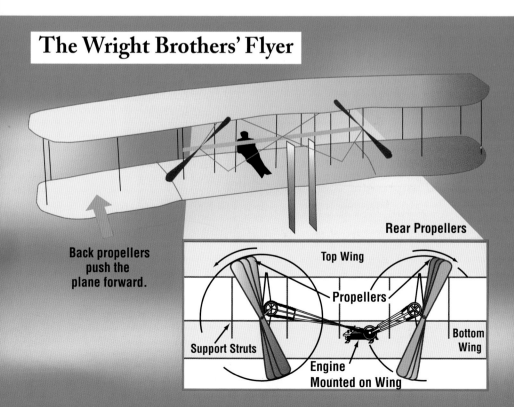

The Wright Brothers' Flyer

Back propellers push the plane forward.

Rear Propellers

Top Wing

Propellers

Support Struts

Engine Mounted on Wing

Bottom Wing

and crash into the sand, damaging its left wing. After two days of repairs, the plane was again ready.

On Thursday, December 17, with freezing temperatures and winds of up to 27 miles per hour, they attempted another flight. It was Orville's turn. To record the event, they focused their camera on the end of the run. Orville ran the engine to heat it properly, and he was off. With a 40-foot run, the aircraft lifted. It reached a height of 10 feet, traveled 120 feet, and flew 12 seconds. There were three more flights that day. The longest was Wilbur's at 852 feet with an airborne time of 59 seconds and a speed of 31 miles per hour.

The Wright brothers had successfully designed, built, and tested their motorized aircraft, but they needed a place closer to home to continue their work, because there was still much work to do.

More Firsts

The Wright brothers returned to Dayton and looked for land nearby to use as a flying field. They bought the one hundred-acre Huffman Prairie, just outside of Dayton. With this new location, they were able to spend more time working on their aircraft, named the Wright Flyer, and improving their flying skills.

Flying was still a learning experience. But as they continued to practice, they gained skill. By the end of the following summer, they logged flights of a quarter mile. But up until this time all of their flights were in a straight line.

On September 20, 1904, Wilbur flew his first circle. The flight covered 4,080 feet and lasted ninety seconds.

A boy runs for cover as a plane flies over him in this illustration from a Christmas card.

The Wrights did not stop there, though. They continued to improve their designs.

By summer's end of 1905, the Wright Flyer III had logged more than forty miles. It could fly several miles at a time and make sharp turns. On October 5, 1905, Wilbur made a flight of nearly forty minutes, turning thirty circles.

Another first for the Wright Flyer III was a cross-country flight in the fall of 1905. The craft flew over

Wilbur Wright is in position to work the controls of his aircraft in 1903.

Dayton and circled their home on Hawthorne Street. People came out of office buildings and homes to watch, and factories blew their whistles.

The Wright brothers had developed aircraft that were stable, maneuverable, and could travel long distances. Now they wanted to market and sell them.

More Success, Accidents, and Endings

The Wright brothers had completed more than forty successful flights, and they wanted to put their aircraft to practical use. But to protect their interests, the Wright brothers got a **patent** for their designs. This kept other people from making money by building and selling aircraft like the Wright Flyer. The brothers offered it to the U.S. War Department, but it had already spent lots of money financing experimental aircraft of other aviators, and it had little if anything to show for the money. Because of the lack of interest shown by the U.S. government, the Wrights looked to other countries.

Between 1906 and 1908, the Wright brothers traveled from the United States to Europe several times with their latest flying machine, the Type A Flyer. It was a two-seater and was controlled by levers instead of the hip cradle control used in their previous aircraft. Also, the new flyer was more powerful. With so much interest in the Wright brothers' aircraft on both sides of the Atlantic, Orville attended demonstrations in the United States while Wilbur worked in Europe.

Carriage drivers and passengers stop to stare at Orville Wright as he flies over them in his glider.

In June 1908, Wilbur opened the shipping cartons in Le Mans, France, where he was going to assemble the flyer. He was shocked to see that nearly all of the parts had been damaged in shipment. It took seven weeks to make all of the repairs and assemble the flyer, but finally on August 8, it was ready for demonstrations. Before a large crowd at a local racetrack, Wilbur took off. He flew for one minute and forty-five seconds and made several banked turns, something never seen before in France. Also during these demonstrations, he gave a ride to Madame Berg, the wife of one of his French hosts. She became the first woman to fly in an aircraft. Orville and Wilbur Wright had fame beyond their dreams, but soon

A crowd shuffles into a racetrack in France to witness a flying demonstration in 1908.

Assistants rush to the aid of Orville Wright after he crash-landed in 1908. His passenger did not survive the accident.

an event occurred that reminded both brothers that flying was still dangerous.

Orville was flying demonstrations for the U.S. Army at Fort Meyer. During one of his last scheduled demonstration flights, he took with him Thomas Selfridge, a twenty-six-year-old lieutenant. In the beginning the flight was routine, but then Orville heard two thumps and the plane began to shake. The left wing dropped and the nose pulled down. Despite Orville's efforts to stay aloft, the plane crashed. Selfridge was rushed to the hospital, but died of his injuries. This was the first death resulting from the flight of a heaver-than-air craft. Orville was seriously injured, as well. When Orville recovered enough to travel, his sister, Katharine, took him to Europe to join their brother.

The Wright brothers' aircraft was so famous that royalty visited the hangar where the flyer was housed in Pau, France. Their success grew steadily and their planes sold in France and Italy; Germany showed an interest in their aircraft, also.

When the Wrights returned to the United States in the summer of 1909, it was to a hero's welcome. Ten thousand people crowded the streets of Dayton on June 17 as the Wrights rode through the city in a parade. The parties and ceremonies went on for two days.

A painting expresses the serenity of flight through a cloudy sky.

Continuing the Flight Business

The Wrights had airplane factories in the United States and in Europe. They were wealthy businessmen, no longer researchers and experimenters. They dealt with pilot training, sales, and lawsuits for copyright violations. They had little time to fly, and sadly one of the brothers had only a short time to live.

On May 30, 1912, at age forty-five, Wilbur Wright died from typhoid fever.

Orville managed the company for a while, but by 1915 he was tired of it. He sold the business and returned to his first love, research. He moved with his father and his sister to a large home just outside Dayton called Hawthorne Hill. Bishop Wright died in 1917 and Katharine married and left home in the 1920s. Orville remained in the house until his death at age seventy-six on January 30, 1948. He had lived to see millions of people transported around the world, thanks to his and Wilbur's invention.

Notes

Chapter 1: The Bishop's Family

1. Quoted in Tom Crouch, *The Bishop's Boys: A Life of Wilbur and Orville Wright*. New York: W.W. Norton, 1989, p. 57

2. Quoted in Crouch, *The Bishop's Boys*, p. 77.

Chapter 2: Brothers in Business

3. Quoted in Crouch, *The Bishop's Boys*, p. 103.

4. Quoted in Crouch, *The Bishop's Boys*, p. 107.

Chapter 3: Taking to the Skies

5. Quoted in Harry Combs, *Kill Devil Hill: Discovering the Secret of the Wright Brothers*. Boston: Houghton Mifflin, 1979, p. 53

6. Quoted in Fred Howard, *Wilbur and Orville: The Story of the Wright Brothers*. New York: Alfred A. Knopf, 1987, p. 39.

7. Quoted in Stephen Kirk, *First in Flight: The Wright Brothers in North Carolina*. Winston-Salem, NC: J.F. Blair, 1995, p. 31.

Chapter 4: Flight and Beyond

8. Quoted in Kirk, *First in Flight*, p. 168.

Glossary

airfoil: A shape that causes more air to travel across its top surface than its bottom surface. Movement of air in this manner creates lift.

biplane: An aircraft that has two wings, one above the other.

depression: A condition in which a person has strong feelings of stress and sadness.

engraving: Carving designs into a surface.

glider: An aircraft that travels on thermals (air currents) without a motor.

patent: A document that makes it illegal for any other person to create and sell a product without the permission of the person who invented or developed the product.

propeller: Airfoils that turn through the air, forcing air over an airplane's wings.

spar: The skeleton of an airplane's wing that gives the wing its strength.

tuberculosis: A disease caused by bacteria that affects the lungs more often than any other organ.

typhoid fever: A disease caused by bacteria that affects the intestines and can also attack the bloodstream.

wing warping: Changing the shape of an airplane's wing to keep the plane balanced in the air.

For Further Exploration

Russell Freedman, *The Wright Brothers: How They Invented the Airplane.* New York: Holiday House, 1991. This biography focuses primarily on the adult lives of the Wright brothers. Some of the black-and-white photographs were actually taken by the Wright brothers.

Spencer Johnson, *The Value of Patience: The Story of the Wright Brothers.* La Jolla, CA: Value Communications, 1976. A fablelike, cartoon-illustrated volume.

Stephen Krensky, *Taking Flight: The Story of the Wright Brothers.* New York: Simon and Schuster, 2000. This is a large-print, colorfully illustrated biography.

Wendie C. Old, *The Wright Brothers: Inventors of the Airplane.* Berkeley Heights, NJ: Enslow, 2000. A fact-filled biography, illustrated in black and white, with a comprehensive chronology.

Index

Picture Credits

Cover photo: Mary Evans Picture Library
Associated Press, AP, 13, 21
Associated Press, The Daily Press, 25
© Bettmann/CORBIS, 6
© Hulton/Archive by Getty Images, 23, 39
Mary Evans Picture Library, 18
Brandy Noon, 27, 33
© North Wind Picture Archives, 38
© Gianni Dagli Orti/CORBIS, 9
PhotoDisc, 7
© Smithsonian Institution, 37
© Stock Montage, Inc., 17, 36
© Patrick Ward/CORBIS, 30
Wright State University, 10, 19, 28, 29, 35, 40

About the Author

Sheila Wyborny is a retired science and social studies teacher living in Houston, Texas, with her husband of more than thirty years. She likes to read in her spare time, and she and her husband enjoy taking trips in their airplane, named Lucy.